Carry Me Home

Carry Me Home

Louisiana Sugar Country photographs by Debbie Fleming Caffery

WITH ESSAYS BY PETE DANIEL AND ANNE WILKES TUCKER

SMITHSONIAN INSTITUTION PRESS WASHINGTON AND LONDON

Library of Congress Cataloging-in-Publication Data

Caffery, Debbie Fleming.

Carry me home : Lousiana sugar country in photographs / by Debbie Fleming Caffery.

p.   cm

Includes bibliographical references (p.   ).

ISBN 0-87474-311-7

1. Sugar workers—Louisiana—Pictorial works.

2. Sugar workers—Louisiana—History.

I. Title.

HD8039.S86U573   1990

331.7'6361'09763—dc20   90-32911   CIP

British Library Cataloguing-in-Publications Data is available

Manufactured in the United States of America

97 96 95 94 93 92 91 90   5 4 3 2 1

♾ The paper used in this publication meets the minimum requirements of the American National Standard for Permanence of Paper for Printed Library Materials Z39.48-1984

Designed by Lisa Buck Vann

Edited by Jennifer Lorenzo

Production managed by Kathleen Brown

Typeset in Joanna by Monotype Composition Company, Inc., Baltimore, Maryland

Printed by South China Printing Company, Hong Kong

Swing low, sweet chariot,

Comin' for to carry me home,

I look over Jordan and what do I see,

Comin' for to carry me home,

A band of angels comin' after me,

Comin' for to carry me home.

TRADITIONAL

CONTENTS

Dedicated with love to Joshua, Ruth, Brennan,
Clegg, Mi Mi, Grandaddy, and Pete Daniel

CKNOWLEDGMENTS

Special thanks are due to Anne Tucker, Marie Martin, Arthur Rogers, Susan Morgan, Anne Petersen, Arthur Ollman, David Kiehl, Episcopal School of Acadiana, Catherine Dietlein, Lynell Comeaux, Thelma Abraham, Josephine Sacabo, Dalt Wonk, Mary Caesar, Reverend John Harris, Polly Joseph, Billy Patout, Employees of M. A. Patout, Hilton Legnon, David Stewart, Jim and Beth DeWoody, Derek Gordon, Marilyn and Bob Tarpy, Anne and Walter Dobie, Brenda London, Miriam Rose, Michael Ray Conner, Michael Dufy, James and Susan Edmunds, Jackie and Conrad Comeaux, Robert Smith, Geoff Winningham and Dawn Frederick.

DEBBIE FLEMING CAFFERY

CONTRIBUTORS

Pete Daniel is a curator in the Division of Agriculture and Natural Resources in the National Museum of American History. He is the author of the prizewinning book *Breaking The Land: The Transformation of Cotton, Tobacco, and Rice Cultures since 1880*, and of *Standing at the Crossroads: Southern Life in the Twentieth Century*. Daniel has also contributed to *Official Images: New Deal Photography*.

Anne Wilkes Tucker is the Gus & Lyndall Wortham curator of photography at the Museum of Fine Arts, Houston, and the author of several books on the history of photography. Like the photographer, Tucker was raised near a sugar plantation in southern Louisiana.

DEEP EXPOSURES: THE LANDSCAPE AND ATMOSPHERE OF MYSTERY · PETE DANIEL

When Debbie Fleming Caffery trains her camera on south Louisiana, she is drawn into a rich history that includes slavery, Civil War, economic cycles of boom and bust, tenancy, labor strikes, and mechanization. Much as William Faulkner turned the stories he heard around Oxford, Mississippi, into fiction, Caffery frames shapes and shadows to suggest themes that often transcend the apparent subject matter. Like Faulkner, she is careful not to reveal too much, leaving room for mystery. The magic in her images comes from her ability to suggest the history and culture that is stored in layers around her. Her subjects, primarily African-Americans who live nearby, exude power and confidence, but they also withhold and conceal, perpetuating the legacy of reticence and separation that typified slavery and segregation and survived even the civil rights movement. Despite the close proximity in housing and in work, African-Americans and whites guard their separate traditions.

13

The culture of the sugar country where Debbie Caffery works, so vividly treated by such novelists as George Washington Cable, Kate Chopin, and Ernest J. Gaines, and more recently analyzed by folklorist Nicholas Spitzer, has intrigued if not fascinated observers for years. Cajun music has gained well-deserved national attention recently, and restaurants from coast to coast offer approximations of Cajun dishes. South Louisiana contains a host of peculiar customs that make it distinct both from other parts of Louisiana and from the nation at large. The region has strong unifying traditions—the sugar culture, the French language, the Roman Catholic religion, festivals, foods, and material culture. Saint Mary Parish, where Debbie Caffery lives, however, has been dominated more by Anglo and African-American culture than by the surrounding Cajun culture. In architecture, language, and religion it more resembles the old lowland South than Creole Caribbean-style French Louisiana.[1]

Once the common elements are defined and a more exacting examination of the region is made, the elements of diversity begin to outweigh those of commonality. Louisiana French, for example, varies from the sugar country to the prairie to New Orleans, each version distinct in inflection and grammar. Although Catholicism dominates the area, Saint Mary Parish has a strong Protestant tradition among the Anglo-planter leadership.[2] The most notable festival is the Mardi Gras of New Orleans, but many towns in south Louisiana have smaller celebrations featuring unique local customs. Food likewise varies, as does folk housing. Throughout south Louisiana waves of settlers for hundreds of years have exchanged myriad traditions, producing the contemporary rich layering of cultures.

Native Americans claimed the area before Europeans settled there some three hundred years ago. Early European arrivals in the eighteenth century, French and German farmers, built on the high ground near the rivers and bayous, which provided transportation to move their indigo and tobacco to market. The Acadians (who were to become known as Cajuns), exiled from Nova Scotia by the British, began arriving after 1765. By the era of the American Revolution, then, Louisiana contained a significant mixture of cultures, including a large number of African slaves.

The Louisiana Purchase in 1803 brought the developing sugar region under the sovereignty of the United States, and although American settlers flocked in, other immigrants had a more powerful impact on the culture. From 1791 through 1809, slave revolts and turmoil in Haiti, Santo Domingo, and other parts of the West Indies prompted white planters to flee with their slaves; many found refuge in Louisiana. These immigrants had more in common with the French and Spanish residents than with the Americans, who brought their own cultural heritage to the area. Creoles of color, an intermediate class of free blacks under the French, lost status because Americans considered all people of African heritage inferior. Nevertheless, African culture, reshaped by the West Indian slave experience, exerted a profound influence on south Louisiana. As Nicholas Spitzer has pointed out, these slaves "profoundly affected south Louisiana architecture (Creole cottages, shotgun houses and wraparound porches), music (Caribbean rhythmic influence on zydeco, old-time jazz and New Orleans street music), food (gumbo, red beans and rice), religion (persistence of voodoo) and language (further emphasis on a Caribbean type of French Creole language)."

Despite the diversity of the residents' origins, no one visiting south Louisiana can ignore the dominance of Cajun culture, which has absorbed or influenced others disproportionately. The cultural layers continue to build in south Louisiana, and in recent years Texas oil workers and Vietnamese fishermen have contributed.[3]

Although this brief tour of south Louisiana suggests the complex cultural background of the sugarcane country where Debbie Caffery works, a deeper sense of mystery pervades the landscape. While touring Belair Plantation in south Louisiana in 1886, *Century* correspondent Eugene V. Smalley became obsessed with what he saw. "The atmosphere," he observed, "is like that in Corot's pictures, misty, vague, and dreamy. The gigantic live oaks seem like ghosts of trees." He sensed that objects and people seemed distorted. "The figures of men and animals moving across the shrouded fields against the gray sky loom into strangely exaggerated proportions." He learned from his planter informants that the African-Americans who lived in the quarters were religious but that some "old heathen superstitions," such as voodoo, persisted.[4] By getting his information from the planters, Smalley perpetuated the perception of African-American culture as exotic: because the planters could not penetrate the private lives of their workers, they would easily mistake voodoo for African-American superstition instead of understanding it as part of the larger religious structure.

In *The Creoles of Louisiana*, published in 1884, George Washington Cable also suggested the mystery and foreboding that seeped from the landscape. "The scenery of this land, where it is still in its wild state," he wrote, "is weird and funereal." He emphasized the special light characteristic of the area: "Even when the forests close in upon the banks of the stream there is a wild and solemn beauty in the shifting scene which appeals to the imagination with special strength when the cool morning lights or the warmer glows of evening impart the colors of the atmosphere to the surrounding wilderness, and to the glassy waters of the narrow and tortuous bayous that move among its shadows." His description was ripe with images of gloom: "dark, pall-like curtains of moss-draped swamp," the "phantomlike arms of lofty cypresses," the "wide-spread silence," a "flock of roosting vultures," or an "alligator crossing the stream."[5] These passages resonate with Debbie Caffery's use of morning light in her photographs and the possibilities for creativity that she finds in the bold shadows and sudden light that cloak or reveal her subjects.

Smalley and Cable wrote their impressions roughly a century after the sugar culture began in Louisiana and almost a century before Debbie Caffery began her work there. While the history of the cane-growing area is extremely important in understanding its peculiar place in southern agricultural and social history, a lengthy treatment is beyond the scope of this essay. Still, a brief review should furnish a helpful perspective and provide the historical context for Caffery's work.

In 1794, a year after the invention of the cotton gin (which led to the spread of cotton and slavery across the South), fifty-four-year-old Etienne de Boré first successfully granulated sugar in Louisiana. Other farmers, desperate to find a crop to replace indigo, threw their resources into sugar production.[6] Thereafter, the fortunes of Louisiana cane growers rose and fell in rhythm with world demand, labor costs, tariff protection, weather, and cane diseases. Sugar production linked south Louisiana to a global market and increased its kinship to the West Indies, where most of the world's sugar was grown. Sugar growers quickly became sugar planters and surrounded themselves with slaves, mansions, and other trappings of aristocracy.

From the beginning there was a sharp division between fieldwork and the operation of the sugar mill. Planting, hoeing, and cutting cane had always been labor intensive, while working in the more mechanized mill called for different talents. In addition to the sugar boilers, carpenters, masons, and other skilled workers were employed.[7] In most cases, whites held the most skilled jobs in the mill and blacks did the fieldwork. The South, usually portrayed as technologically backward, kept abreast of the latest advances in sugar mills, cotton gins, and rice mill design. As early as 1822, a Louisiana planter adopted steam-processing equipment, and by 1838 only Pennsylvania had more operating steam engines than Louisiana.[8] By 1861, 1,027 of the 1,291 sugar houses in the state used steam. The energy devoted to invention focused on the sugar mills—not the fields.[9]

Throughout the antebellum period, planters searched for more economical ways to extract sugar from cane. The process, succinctly explained by historian John Alfred Heitmann, has five major steps: "grinding the cane; defecating and purifying the extracted juice; evaporating the juice to a viscous syrup, granulating the syrup, with the formation of sugar crystals; and potting, the separation of crystals and molasses by slow drainage."[10] Some planters blamed African-Americans for preventing even more rapid technological advances, arguing that slaves were incapable of learning the operation of complex sugar machinery. In fact, historians have suggested, slaves often broke implements and machines or feigned ignorance as a means of resistance. What could appear to the master's eye as ineptitude or clumsiness could in reality be shrewdly calculated sabotage. Some planters, no doubt, consigned black workers to the fields, convinced that a broken plow, hoe, or cane knife was more easily replaced than a steam engine.

Norbert Rillieux, a Creole of color born in 1806, personified African-American inventiveness and countered the stereotype of ineptitude. He graduated from the Ecole Polytechnique in Paris and became intrigued by steam power, which he hoped to harness for sugar refining. For years after his return to Louisiana he experimented on vacuum evaporation. At last in 1843 he patented his invention, which Heitmann described as "the premier engineering achievement in nineteenth-century sugar technology." Heitmann suggested that it was "ironic and one of the many paradoxes of the Old South that many planters argued that an evaporator invented by the black scientist Rillieux was too complicated to be operated by black men."[11] Such misconceptions grew out of the dynamics of slavery, in which whites looked for subservience and passivity and blacks retreated behind a line of defenses that protected their evolving culture from prying white eyes. No wonder whites thought that slave behavior was inexplicable.

The Civil War also decimated the sugar business. In 1861 the South produced 459,410 hogsheads of sugar valued at $25 million; three years later it produced only 10,000 hogsheads valued at $2 million. More important, emancipation erased $100 million invested in slaves.[12] Yet whites retained control over former slaves. During the war the occupying Union military yielded to planters' demands and set up a contract system that, while granting workers concessions that prohibited whipping and kept families together, curtailed freedom of movement.[13]

It took years for the sugar industry to rebuild after the war, and in desperation some farmers turned briefly to growing cotton. Despite the turmoil, by 1870 production had picked up to 144,881 hogsheads and by 1879 it reached 213,000.[14] Planters, apprehensive about controlling the labor of free blacks, attempted to attract Germans, Italians, Chinese, and other groups to work in the cane fields. Although by 1900 there were some one thousand immigrants employed in the cane area, planters continued to rely principally on African-Americans.[15] Most planters hired workers on wages and furnished housing in "the quarters," a row of small houses. Planters and workers bargained constantly over wages and perquisites, as freedom allowed a more direct protest than sabotage.

During the last quarter of the nineteenth century, sugarcane workers struck for higher wages in 1880 and in 1887. In both cases the state militia supported the planters' interests. The Knights of Labor organized the 1887 strike, which ended in violence as armed white vigilantes in Thibodaux killed at least thirty cane workers. The strike was broken, and workers cut cane for the planters' price.[16] The cultural gulf between the

black and white populations remained because whites no more understood the hopes and aspirations of blacks as their free neighbors than
they had of them as slaves.

In 1877, even before the labor unrest, Louisiana planters founded
the Louisiana Sugar Planters' Association. The group lobbied successfully
for higher tariff rates and set up a sugar exchange to regulate marketing
among planters and brokers on the New Orleans levee. More important
was the need to transfer the sophisticated chemical and technological
breakthroughs of German sugar beet refining, which were far beyond the
grasp of most planters. To transfer those ideas to Louisiana and adapt
them to cane would require university-trained scientists.[17] After some
false starts, the U.S. Department of Agriculture founded an experiment
station in 1885 at Louisiana State University. The hit-or-miss methods of
growing and purifying sugarcane largely ended as science and technology
combined to regulate sugar production. Increasingly the growing and the
manufacturing of sugar separated into distinct areas of study.[18]

The sugar industry prospered until 1912 but then declined due to
floods, early frosts, unfavorable tariff duties, cane diseases, and poor
cultivation practices. Hard times led to the consolidation of sugar mills,
and their number fell from some 300 in 1900 to fewer than 200 ten years
later; by 1926 only 54 survived. Fieldwork also changed as tenants
increasingly replaced wage hands. Many cane workers left during World

War I, either to join the armed forces or to seek better employment opportunities elsewhere. In the 1920s an outbreak of mosaic destroyed crops, in 1924 anthrax killed some 20,000 head of livestock, and in 1927 a devastating flood ruined much of the crop. As a result, planters abandoned cultivation and many cane workers moved away.[19]

Debbie Caffery, like most residents of south Louisiana, grew up aware of this history, but not everyone understood the cycle of work that produced sugar. Debbie became fascinated with the sugar mill across the bayou from her home in New Iberia. Yet it was only in 1974, when she was a student at the San Francisco Art Institute and received a work-study grant that she spent the entire grinding season in the fields and sugar mills. She has returned time and again and is now accepted by the cane workers as one engaged in her own labors in the cycle of cultivation and harvest.

Understanding the work cycle of sugar cultivation and how it has changed over time helps in interpreting Caffery's photographs. In the spring of 1988 Lu Ann Jones, who has been conducting oral-history interviews for the National Museum of American History's Oral History of Southern Agriculture project, spent several weeks in south Louisiana talking to people involved in the sugar culture. Jessie A. Breaux, Sr., Reverend John Harris, and Florentine Daniel, three workers who spent most of their lives working in the sugar culture near Franklin, and Andrew

Gay, who is president of the Saint Louis Plantation near Plaquemine, provided rare insight into the forces of continuity and change.

They revealed the routines of daily life, the seasonal work in the cane fields and at the sugar mills, and commented on how mechanization and chemicals have altered the way cane workers earn their living. Their memories go back to the era of the Great Depression, and collectively they construct a context for much of Caffery's work, for they have lived through a significant transformation in the way cane is grown, cultivated, harvested, and processed. Much of Caffery's photography is tied to the daily and seasonal routines of cane workers. "Thirty, forty of us going out in the field with cane knives, hoes, plows—name it," says one of Ernest J. Gaines's characters in *A Gathering of Old Men*. "Sunup to sundown, hard, miserable work, but we managed to get it done."[20] Tradition runs deep in cane country.

The Breaux family, like many other Cajuns in the area, had been involved in the sugar culture for generations. "Was Dozeit Breaux, my great-great-grandfather," Jessie Breaux recounted. "And then my grandfather, Lewis Breaux, he was there. And then my daddy. And then from there, took it from footstep to footstep." His two sons are in the sugar business also. "So, to them, that's be about the fifth or sixth generation in the sugar. That's way back yonder."[21]

The Reverend John Harris also followed in his father's footsteps.

When he was about fourteen years old, he drove a two-wheeled water cart and delivered water and food to the field crew; in 1940 he became field supervisor. Like his father before him, who preached until he was eighty-eight years old, the Reverend Harris was called to be a preacher, and like his father he at first resisted the call. "But it looked like I was cracking up. Looked like I was losing my mind, until something spoke to me and said, 'I want you to get up. I want you to preach.' "[22] When he decided it was time to have a photograph of himself, he called on Caffery, who obliged with a powerful yet subtle image of Reverend Harris in front of his church holding his Bible.

Florentine Daniel was born in 1913, and she was baptized by Reverend Harris's father. She started working in the cane fields when she was fourteen years old. "See," she explained, "I didn't get a learning," adding that she only attended school on "them days I felt like it."[23]

Andrew Gay's family arrived in sugar country in 1805, just in time to take advantage of the sugar boom. As a boy Gay rode his horse through the fields. "I knew all the workers by name and practically all the mules," he recalled. "So I've always had an interest in the operation of the plantation." After World War II, Gay returned from the military and began managing Saint Louis Plantation, in his words, "carrying on a tradition." In 1948 he closed the plantation sugar mill, declaring that "it was old and inadequate."[24]

Before mechanization, all four people remembered, mules did the draft work in the sugar culture, much as they did in cotton and tobacco cultivation. Keeping mules dictated to some degree the physical appearance of a sugar farm. Farmers grew corn to feed them and built barns to house them, and kept collars, hames, trace chains, single trees, lines, plows, harrows, and other cultivating implements. The labor-intensive nature of using stock instead of machines meant that fieldwork had a certain rhythm.

For people who live in the sugar culture, the year is marked by the seasons. In late summer cane is planted in the open fields. Then, beginning around the first of October, mature cane planted in earlier seasons is cut and refined, a process called grinding that lasts into December. In the spring and summer the growing cane is cultivated by plow and weeded. Over time the seasonal tasks have changed, primarily due to machines and chemicals that have largely replaced human labor.

The daily work routine, Jessie Breaux said, started with a wake-up bell that rang at 4:30 in the morning; then, at 5:30 a second bell called people to the fields. Breaux often rang the bell. "First thing in the morning, I'd get on that bell and I'd hang on it. I'd ring it like hell." While some people teased Breaux that they were still in bed when the second bell rang, Florentine Daniel remembered that "we would get up early, sometime before that first bell would ring and do a lot of work in the house before you go to work." No matter what the season, she would prepare a noon meal and at night wash clothes.[25] Debbie Caffery rises to her own bell and eagerly awaits first light, when the shapes of workers, tools, machines, and cane materialize in the mist and fires of daybreak.

In the spring and summer, workers formerly used hoes to chop out the grass in the cane fields. Jessie Breaux remembered that "sometimes they had a hundred people string out hoeing."[26] Chopping ended, Reverend Harris explained, when "the farmers in Baton Rouge come up with a chemical to kill the grass in the cane. They poison it. You see out there. You don't see no grass in that cane. . . . At harvest time you still won't see no grass. That's how they got rid of all the hoes. . . . You don't see a hoe now unless you see it around somebody's house."[27]

Fields are not planted every year because cane will grow back and produce sugar for several years. The first planting is called "plant cane," and when it grows back after cutting it is called "stubble." Jessie Breaux explained that "you make sometimes three or four crop on that one plant of plant cane." According to Andrew Gay, the cane "grows as much as an inch and a half a day in the summer. It's amazing."[28] Florentine Daniel's first fieldwork was planting cane. In the 1920s, she remembered, "they had mens on each side of a wagon dropping the cane. And you'd get behind with a cane knife and straighten that what didn't fall, straighten the crooked cane." Now automatic planters do this work.[29]

Grinding season mobilized the entire work force both in the fields and at the sugar mill. During harvest in the days before mechanical harvesters, workers streamed into the area from nearby parishes. "They'd go out there and pick up two truckload of people and bring 'em down here and they put 'em in the boarding house," Jessie Breaux remembered. "They had their bunk bed for 'em, mattress and everything they needed, right there for 'em."[30]

Workers were in the fields by sunrise, usually standing near a fire fueled by cane shucks or old tires. Andrew Gay recalled that at Saint Louis Plantation "there would literally be one hundred or more people strung out on . . . a road where the rows begin, each assigned to a row. . . . Sometimes it would take almost a day to cut a single row."[31] The work fell into a rhythm. "You catch that cane, pull it to you," Reverend Harris explained. "Catch it with this hand, you flag it, knock the flags off of it. You top it. . . . And when you top them, you grab 'em, you cut 'em close to ground. Got to cut the stubble in the ground. Then you put it across a heap row." Although the work was hard, Harris said that "them people, mens and women, they'd laugh and talk and sing all day." Before machines "you were using sometime a hundred, a hundred-twenty-five knives, cutting cane. Right now, you take two harvesters'll cut as much as them one hundred and twenty-five knives."[32]

Both men and women worked in the fields. "When it come down

to harvesting the cane for the sugar mill," Florentine Daniel remembered, "they'd have mens and women. At that time we used to cut cane by hand, all the way through." She preferred fieldwork to housework. "I loved the fieldwork. . . . I loved to get out there and make a day's work and come on back to the house." Andrew Gay insisted that "women, as a whole, could cut cane better than men, or they would cut cane better and more rapidly than men."[33]

By World War II these labor practices were beginning to change. In addition to tractors and cane harvesters, hoeing machines, stubble diggers, cane pilers, and field loaders could be seen against the horizon. During the 1930s farmers sought better cane varieties, and despite New Deal production quotas, by 1938 production had reached 490,000 tons.[34]

World War II also radically changed the labor situation in the sugar area. For one thing, the Department of Agriculture removed quotas and allowed unlimited production. This plus military service and the attraction of defense work strained the labor supply. Sugar planters desperately looked for workers, hoping at first to use Japanese-American interns from Arkansas, then German prisoners of war, or migrant laborers, or even local loiterers. In October 1943 the rule that forbade prisoner-of-war camps within 150 miles of the coast was waived, and more than a half-dozen camps sprang up in cane country. Reverend Harris remembered the German prisoners well, for he worked with some of the 237 from the camp in Franklin. By the 1944 season there were nearly 5,000 POWs in Louisiana.[35] In 1953 the National Agricultural Workers Union organized a strike, but even the legendary H. L. Mitchell, who had organized the Southern Tenant Farmers Union in the 1930s, could not inspire success. In some ways the 1953 strike resembled strikes of the 1880s, except that in this case the Catholic Church actively sided with the workers.[36]

The cane country, like other agricultural commodity areas, continued to transform as the forces of science and technology accelerated after the war. Reverend John Harris recalled in May 1988 that when he first saw tractors, "I noticed it was cutting out a lot of people from working, 'cause you take one tractor could plow more in a day than eight men with mules. The tractors cut out a lot of labor." Florentine Daniel remembered being excited when the machines appeared. "Then when they started with the cane cutters, it was more excitement to us, to see a machine was doing what we would do."[37]

Many of the workers who have remained in the area are not only victims of mechanization but subject to fluctuations in the oil industry as well. The 1970 census showed that in Saint Mary Parish 46.3 percent of the families live below the government poverty level. Although part of the cause of poverty lies outside the sugar culture, much is a result of mechanization. In that sense south Louisiana shares many of the problems of other agricultural areas that formerly required a large labor force. The forces of contraction and consolidation also affected planters. In 1953 there were more than 4,000 farms producing sugar, but in 1973 only 1,290 remained.[38] The sugar culture, like most of American agriculture, has substituted machines and chemicals for human power and, as aggressive farmers absorb weaker rivals, the displaced workers have been in many cases discarded and forgotten.

Andrew Gay suggested that the workers "just kind of disappeared into the woodwork." Some worked for sawmills or in construction while others found jobs with petrochemical firms—"or else they just kind of one by one left, either got employment somewhere or else they became of an age where they could draw certain benefits and not need to work on a plantation."[39]

The sugar culture that Debbie Caffery found in the mid-1970s was far into reliance on science and technology. She was witness to an era of significant transformation in rural life, and she sought to understand it through her camera. When she started her work on the sugar culture, she suspected that she was working on a dying way of life, but she discovered the resilience of the culture that even now continually advances and retreats, experiments with new techniques, and occasionally calls in hand labor. The older workers, as well as those who retired, preserve the memory of a venerable but extinct work process. Caffery stands with one foot in the past and the other in the present, her camera registering this ambivalent but powerful stance. It is as if by opening the shutter she coaxes atmosphere and magic into the film.

Caffery watches and listens and allows her curiosity to drive her to the fields and sugar mills where year after year she finds fresh images that delve into the mystery and confusion of the past. She has captured images of daily and seasonal routines that have evolved over two centuries and that even in the machine and chemical age have left traces of a complex culture. Her photographs convey a sense of place, mood, and timelessness that elevate them above the ordinary.

NOTES

1. Nicholas Spitzer, "Les Américains: Anglos in South Louisiana," 252–74; "Afro-Americans in South Louisiana" 276–300, in *The Mississippi Delta Ethnographic Overview*, ed. Spitzer (New Orleans: Jean Lafitte National Historical Park, 1979). On Cajun culture, see William Faulkner Rushton, *The Cajuns: From Acadia to Louisiana* (New York: Farrar Straus Giroux, 1979); James H. Dorman, *The People Called Cajuns: An Introduction to an Ethnohistory* (Lafayette: University of Southwestern Louisiana, 1983).

2. Spitzer, "Les Américains: Anglos in South Louisiana," 266.

3. Nicholas Spitzer, "South Louisiana: Unity and Diversity in a Folk Region," in *Louisiana Folklife: A Guide to the State*, ed. Spitzer (Baton Rouge: Louisiana Department of Culture, Recreation, and Tourism, 1985), 75–82.

4. Eugene V. Smalley, "Sugar-Making in Louisiana," *Century*, November 1887, 101–2.

5. George Washington Cable, *The Creoles of Louisiana* (New York: Charles Scribner's Sons, 1884), 6–7.

6. Ibid., 108–13.

7. J. Carlyle Sitterson, *Sugar Country: The Cane Sugar Industry in the South, 1753–1959* (Lexington: University of Kentucky Press, 1953), 323.

8. John Alfred Heitmann, *The Modernization of the Louisiana Sugar Industry, 1830–1910* (Baton Rouge: Louisiana State University Press, 1987), 32.

9. Sitterson, *Sugar Country*, 138, 226.

10. Heitmann, *Modernization of the Louisiana Sugar Industry*, 10–11.

11. Ibid., 17, 38–39.

12. Sitterson, *Sugar Country*, 226.

13. Thomas Becnel, *Labor, Church, and the Sugar Establishment: Louisiana, 1887–1976* (Baton Rouge: Louisiana State University Press, 1980), 2–3.

14. Sitterson, *Sugar Country*, 251.

15. Ibid., 238–39, 251, 316.

16. William Ivy Hair, *Bourbonism and Agrarian Protest: Louisiana Politics, 1877–1900* (Baton Rouge: Louisiana State University Press, 1971), 171–84.

17. Heitmann, *Modernization of the Louisiana Sugar Industry*, 68–97, 115.

18. Ibid., 137–87, 192–207, 208–43.

19. Sitterson, *Sugar Country*, 344–45, 347, 357–60.

20. Ernest J. Gaines, *A Gathering of Old Men* (New York, Vintage ed., Random House, 1984), 91.

21. Interview with Jessie A. Breaux, Sr., by Lu Ann Jones, Franklin, Louisiana, May 30, 1988, An Oral History of Southern Agriculture, National Museum of American History.

22. Interview with Reverend John Harris, by Lu Ann Jones, Franklin, Louisiana, May 28, 1988, An Oral History of Southern Agriculture, National Museum of American History.

23. Interview with Florentine Daniel, by Lu Ann Jones, Franklin, Louisiana, May 27, 1988, An Oral History of Southern Agriculture, National Museum of American History.

24. Interview with Andrew Gay, by Lu Ann Jones, Plaquemine, Louisiana, May 19, 1988, An Oral History of Southern Agriculture, National Museum of American History.

25. Breaux and Daniel interviews.

26. Breaux interview.

27. Harris interview.

28. Breaux and Gay interviews.

29. Daniel interview.

30. Breaux interview.

31. Gay interview.

32. Harris interview.

33. Daniel and Gay interviews.

34. Sitterson, *Sugar Country*, 382, 387.

35. Harris interview; Becnel, *Labor, Church, and the Sugar Establishment*, 82, 85, 87.

36. Becnel, *Labor, Church, and the Sugar Establishment*, 93–107, 112, 119, 126–39, 150; H. L. Mitchell, *Mean Things Happening in This Land: The Life and Times of H. L. Mitchell, Co-Founder of the Southern Tenant Farmers Union* (Montclair, N.J.: Allanheld, Osmun & Co., 1979), 287–88.

37. Harris and Daniel interviews.

38. Becnel, *Labor, Church, and the Sugar Establishment*, 150, 158, 199, 201–2, 206–7.

39. Gay interview.

"HAVE A FIELD ON MY MIND THAT NEEDS PLOWING"

ANNE WILKES TUCKER

> In the Delta, most of the world seemed sky. The clouds were large—
> larger than horses or houses, larger than boats or churches or gins, larger
> than anything except the fields. . . . The land was perfectly flat and level
> but it shimmered like the wing of a lighted dragonfly. It seemed strummed,
> as though it were an instrument and something had touched it.
>
> —EUDORA WELTY, *DELTA WEDDING*

In 1976 I was thinking of those lines while viewing William Eggleston's exhibition at the Museum of Modern Art in New York City. Most of his photographs were made either in Memphis or in Mississippi, regions I know from childhood trips with my uncle Bill, who was a cotton-scales salesman. I was thinking how downright candid those photographs were about a familiar, dear place when the woman next to me uttered, "This is all so *exotic!*" Texas screenwriter Bud Shrake described a similar

35

36

experience when he said of his film *Songwriter*, "A lot of people called that a black comedy. We just thought it was a documentary."[1]

These experiences encapsule a problem inherent in seeking to describe a minority or provincial culture. What seems natural to members of the community strikes outsiders as exotic and impenetrable, even comic. Feeling baffled, they frequently project the discomfort of incomprehension onto the subject being viewed. Like others who protect their cultural legacies, Southerners relish what is distinctive in their lives and understandably resist the implication that their customs are curious (even freakish) because the viewer finds them alien.

In assaying Debbie Fleming Caffery's photographs, Yale University professor Alan Trachtenberg expressed his own discomfort with the life Caffery portrays. "The Louisiana cane field," he wrote, "seems more truly a world apart, a place and culture of its own, an otherness virtually absolute. Each realm cherishes its own enigmas, its own preserve of buried secrets, but surely it is at the cane field where we perceive ourselves most fully as aliens, outsiders."[2] Born, educated, and employed in New Haven, Trachtenberg finds the sugarcane industry to be a world "left behind" and its culture to be extraneous to modern thought and contemporary urban societies.

The cane industry, however, has always been in the fabric of Caffery's life. She was born in New Iberia, Louisiana, and raised on a bayou across from a sugar mill. Each year of her early childhood she and her grandfather visited the mill during grinding season. Caffery now lives in Franklin, Louisiana, where many of the 8,000 residents are third- and fourth-generation sugar industry managers and workers. Cane fields spread to the horizon beyond Caffery's driveway. After years of decline, surviving mills are expanding their grinding capacities. She passionately hopes that the industry will continue to revive.

Caffery's concern for the sugar industry originally led her to photograph it in 1973 and has sustained her subsequent interest. Yet she doesn't ply her cause with her craft. Her pictures are neither crusading documents on the working conditions of Louisiana cane field workers nor reportage of the industry. She doesn't label or order her photographs to clarify factual connections. Therefore, one cannot read social patterns from her images because single photographs reveal nothing about the frequency of the particular circumstances being photographed. For instance, she primarily photographs black field workers, but this does not necessarily establish that there are not more white or Hispanic employees. Like most photographs—even those coupled with extensive texts—their value as information is greatest for those already familiar with the general subject and thus best able to interpret them.

Nevertheless, there is ample information available to the casual viewer of Caffery's photographs: it is evident that both men and women work in the sugarcane fields, that many field workers are black, and that they use hand tools, such as hoes and cane knives, as well as heavy machinery. The photographs also convey the backbreaking and relentless monotony of harvesting, loading and unloading cane stalks, and stacking bales of bagasse (cane residue) before feeding them into boilers. As Caffery portrays them, the workers possess great vitality. Physical strength and pride are manifest in the way they hold their tools and perform their tasks.

Seasonal conditions are tangible. Cane is harvested in the damp cold of winter's approach. The dampness penetrates protective clothing, making temperatures feel lower. When it's cold and dank, workers wear rubber slickers and knit caps. One young man seems to be wearing a hand-me-down slicker so large he must twist the bib straps across his chest to make the pants fit. When atmospheric winds reverse and come from the Gulf rather than the plains, the long workdays can turn hot and humid. Shirts come off. A man lies in the dusty road tracks, knowing that freshly turned earth is cool. His broad, powerful back relaxes with sleep as his weight settles into the patterned tire impressions. The field stretches past him; leaves of cane stubble catch the early morning light.

Caffery's earliest photographs are her most straightforward records, rich with contextual information and traditionally composed, with the sitter centrally located in the frame. People are Caffery's abiding concern.

Their faces engage the viewer, never confront. These people are not the victims of a hit-and-run photographer. Caffery has known some of them since childhood and has photographed others during grinding season for over a decade.

None of Caffery's pictures conform to traditional landscape genres. Nevertheless, Louisiana vistas figure prominently in her work. South Louisiana soil is moist, dark, fecund, and flat; forests are dense with undergrowth and smell of compost. Bayous and marshy lakes cut the fields. Skies are clear with lazy, white puff clouds, mocking the labor below with their leisure. Or the firmament is dark, rattling with thunder, violent clouds, and the threat of rain. Whether flushed with sun or soaked, the land is laden with emotional intensity. And even if the land is excluded, its presence is an undercurrent—felt. As one distracted overseer told Caffery, "I have a field on my mind that needs plowing."

Religion is another motif in Caffery's work. Its presence is appropriate because worship is an integral part of the cane community. Workers still sing hymns in the fields. An early portrait displays Reverend John Harris in his ministerial robes. Before he retired, Reverend Harris was a cane field overseer and, like his father, is a minister for several small Baptist churches. Given his local esteem in both professions, Harris chose to be portrayed in his rich black robes, standing in front of a whitewashed church rather than in the fields.

Another subtly provocative picture is that of garfish skins hanging over the single word, CHURCH, on a road sign. Maybe someone just wanted to hang the skins out to dry and this sign was the most convenient spot. But Southern belief systems draw on diverse traditions. Besides Episcopal, Methodist, Catholic, and myriad Baptist offshoots, there are heretical groups, including Charismatics, palm readers, Blue Ridge snake cults, and Louisiana voodoo. The scaly, twisted fish skin against the proper municipal symmetry of the sign and its orthodox message is evocative of the uneasy coexistence of established religions and cults in Louisiana.

Caffery's work possesses documentary roots without documentary intentions. Although she is mindful of accuracy, her compelling motivations are aesthetic and emotional. Her work is not "about" the sugarcane industry, just as Malcolm Cowley once observed that Faulkner's *Absalom Absalom!* was "no more intended as a historical account of the country south of Ohio than *The Scarlet Letter* was intended as a history of Massachusetts or *Paradise Lost* as a factual account of the Fall."[3] While Caffery bases her work on a lifelong intimacy with the place and its people, and finds it fruitful to live and work near her sources, she acknowledges that knowing the facts and wanting to display them are separate impulses. "How can I say this?" asked Caffery. "The real world out there is not something I particularly like to deal with."[4]

In her most recent work, Caffery overthrows her previous efforts to be factually informative. Instead, she transforms her subjects in dramatic ways. Sometimes she stands unexpectedly near her sitter, excluding contextual information. One can't fully perceive the person's location or task. The subject is removed both from real time and from any sense of hard times. Caffery's perceptions and feelings overpower the objective evidence. For example, in an untitled photograph made in 1985, Caffery portrays a muscular man with a fleecy gray beard holding a gigantic rabbit. The man is faceless. He is a rabbit breeder standing near his hutches, but the cages are excluded along with all other contextual details. Pictorially, the picture coils as tightly in its frame as both the rabbit and the powerful shoulders of the man are coiled, each tense against the other and against anything unforeseen.

In her search for visually arresting transformation, Caffery also abandons pictorial detail. Sometimes she achieves this by inserting a veil between subject and viewer. Anyone who grew up in the South is familiar with the effect of looking through a screened window or door. Given the South's insect-rich, subtropical climate, wire screens were essential protective barriers before air-conditioning became practical. Screens admit any merciful breeze while keeping bugs batting against the wire. Usually diaphanous, window screens also diffuse the details of the exterior scene, reducing it to hazy shapes. In Caffery's recent photographs, the world is often viewed as though through the screens of childhood. She distills mass and outline from texture. Details melt in swirling smoke or sink into dewy windshields or filmy curtains, leaving only the rhythmic intensity of outlines. What remain are a Sphinx-like head of a seated man, a child agilely climbing a tree, or disembodied legs tramping through a smoking field.

Concurrently, Caffery is drawn to black, the color of mystery, as the dominant tone in her photographs. She photographs in the early hours when day has not yet won the battle with night. "Where I like to photograph now," she explained, "is in really dark places, where there is only minimal light. I respond to the absence of light."

She uses darkness as a piecemeal veil. Within a picture she shifts surprisingly easily from descriptive details, such as a shiny slicker or rusty truck door, to broad areas of black void without orienting details. Reality is simultaneously retained and detached. Retaining salient details keeps the composition from becoming merely a high-contrast design. Scenes take on the quality of a vivid but eerie dream. And like dreams the pictures are open to multiple interpretations. For me, *PaPa* (1986) portrays a bulky man in a fedora towering over the field like a protective totem. His royal robe of smoke billows around him; flames play harmlessly around his feet. This description ascribes mythic properties to the figure and alludes to an ancient, paternal relationship with the land, without any documentary references specifically to sugarcane. In Caffery's reading, she focuses instead on the subject's elegant stance, which becomes emblematic of his profession. "The movement of the smoke around him and the way his whole body seems to flow from his hat to the fire," she decided, "reflects the gracefulness of the sugarmaking process."[5]

Usually Caffery makes darkness penetrable, not perilous but isolating. In *Homage to Wildcat* (1988), the pitch-dark forms are menacing. The black metal jaws of heavy machinery seem to close around the mill itself rather than the cane the machine was designed to gather. The photograph allegorizes the fate of the cane industry. With mechanization, cane harvesting evolved from a labor-intensive industry of many small mills into an agribusiness. Modernized methods of farming sharply reduced the number of jobs. One mechanized cutter replaces 125 field workers with cane knives; chemical weed killers displace the workers who hoed the fields throughout the spring and summer. Families that worked for the same company for generations are now unemployed, work seasonally, or have changed professions. Here, the mill is emblematic of jobs that vanished in the wake of mechanization, and the metal jaws connote how modern economics have devoured many mills.

Caffery is attracted by the fires in the cane fields as well as those in the boiler room of the mill. The workers gather around crackling fires for warmth and harness fires in their work. In the dim light, fires pop out like spiky white altars. Traditionally, fires symbolize transformation.

Perhaps Caffery is wondering whether the cane industry can yet rise renewed from its burning fields.

Caffery's recent style has come most sharply into focus in her photographs of Polly. Since they met in 1984, Debbie has made hundreds of photographs of Polly, of which 30 are now in her portfolio. Polly lives 130 miles away in a shotgun cabin heated by a fireplace and air-conditioned by open windows.* Caffery visits Polly every few months. "I really think that I heightened my sensitivity to black-and-white in her house," said Caffery, "from going back there so many times and then working with the negatives and print tones in the darkroom for so many hours."

Ever since Caffery first saw Polly standing in her yard and stopped to meet her, the two have shared an intense rapport. Each visit, much of their time is spent in long, intimate conversations about each other's lives. Polly's life is shocking in its poverty and isolation, and touching in its search for beauty. Her life-style is not what the media would describe as contemporary. What matters to her is not high-speed, high-tech, or high-priced. Photographer Keith Carter has said of his own photographic subjects in East Texas, "There are a number of these people that have these great lives of the spirit. They work hard in small places to make their lives interesting."[6] Polly's method is to collect things—flowers,

*She recently moved to a nursing home.

weeds, bottles, bits of wood—and from this flotsam and jetsam to construct still lifes both uncalculated and precise. Gathering and arranging them is a sustaining ritual for her.

Something vibrant in Polly's still-life compositions has resonance for Caffery. She photographs Polly's heavy black frying pan, white bowl, and silverware casually laid on a work shirt; a figurine on the mantel; baby shoes on the windowsill; and delicate white lilies laid sweetly on an old-fashioned sewing machine. It was Caffery who brought the flowers and laid them on the machine when Polly had no vase for them. In this instance, Caffery records her own desire to delicately affect the dark interior.

Occasionally, Polly holds something forward as an evocative offering. One May afternoon she held out her rooster; he looks capable of defending their turf. In a photograph made three weeks later, Polly's arm thrusts out a flowering weed with its roots still clinging to the dirt from which it was ripped. The picture is about air, earth, and light gathered in a gentle fist. There is a religious quality to those offerings and to other images of Polly. In one portrait made in 1985, she sits with her dress partially open, exposing her breastbone. A sharp, thrusting beam of light enters diagonally, seeming to pierce her heart like God's fiery spear of divine love pierced Saint Teresa of Avila. Polly's eyes are closed and her head is in motion as though thrown back in ecstasy.

In Polly's home, impenetrable shadows sensuously envelop her. In fact, there is no color in her rooms. They are a study in chiaroscuro; everything is black with smoke from the fireplace. Photographing here is a serious challenge. As in the cane fields at dawn, Caffery wants to maintain a balance between a luxuriant, enveloping darkness and evocative detail. The effort effected a change. "I began to see more in black-and-white," realized Caffery, "past the greenness of the river levee and blue of the sky."

Alan Trachtenberg perceived that Caffery's "camera slashes through darkness, intense in its own seeking of a body to touch, a life to join."[7] Nowhere is this more perceptible than in the pictures of Polly. Her voluminous body dominates Caffery's early portraits and invites associations to figures ranging from fertility idols, such as the Venus of Willendorf, to nurturing, maternal authority figures, such as Ethel Waters's role in Carson McCullers's *The Member of the Wedding*.

Polly is a mysterious "other" with whom Caffery feels kinship despite their vast economic, social, racial, and cultural differences. Nonconformity is paramount among the traits they share. The photographs mined from their relationship confirm their intimate, trusting bond. In this respect, the series is unusual in photography; there are few other sustained series of portraits of an intimate friend except when that person is also the photographer's spouse, lover, or child. The older woman offers herself. The younger repays her with attention. Such heed is a natural and reasonable thing for Polly to want. Caffery bears witness to Polly's existence.

Caffery photographs her own children as well, celebrating the games and riddles of their lives. Some of the pictures are of singularly innocent joys. In *Summer* (1985), a large inner tube rolls downhill toward the river with reckless speed. Braced for the splash, a boy curls expectantly inside the tube. In *May Van's Camp* (1987), Caffery captures the children gossiping under a small tree by the bayou. One child shimmies up the tree while a green lizard climbs the thin window shade in the foreground.

Sometimes, Caffery commemorates her children's youthful imaginations. In one photograph, Ruth, her middle child, casts her shadow in exaggerated size against the wall. When Joshua was bitten by a harmless snake, he responded to the scare by finger painting his body. Caffery photographed his badge of "blood" which is out of proportion to the scale of the encounter except, of course, in Joshua's mind. In another image, a ghost whose ancient garment is frayed and holey is devouring, or maybe embracing, a child on a weathered porch. The child is motionless, not even tense, so it must be a friendly ghost.

Caffery's family is important to her. She ceased to photograph while her children were very young. Clegg Caffery's support of his wife is both emotional and strategic. During the grinding season, he gets the children fed and to school while Debbie rises at 4:30 to photograph. Although she had known Clegg since high school, her photography of the sugarcane industry brought them together in the mid-seventies. When they were married, he moved to San Francisco with her so that she could complete her degree at the San Francisco Art Institute. Clegg speaks with great pride about his wife's accomplishments, such as her recent receipt of the Governor of Louisiana's award for outstanding achievement in the arts.

The governor's award is an important vindication for Debbie Caffery. The white supremacist ideal of southern womanhood may be obsolete, but it is not extinct. The common bias is still for women to fit into traditional stereotypes, and in small towns like Franklin, such biases are easier and less subtly manifest than in a city. Debbie may be a devoted wife and attentive mother, but it is still not considered "fittin' " in the South for a woman to crisscross the countryside by herself just to photograph. Caffery tires of the "bad vibes" she gets from men and women who are as baffled by her artistic drive as Alan Trachtenberg was alienated by the sugarcane culture. Her increasingly successful career as a photographer admits her into artistic circles where she feels refreshingly and predictably comfortable. But these are not proximate communities in space, time, or spirit to her artistic sources: southern Louisiana, its sugarcane industry, Polly, and her family.

There are times when Caffery feels overwhelmed by the complications of trying to balance her responsibilities as a mother, wife, and artist, much less cope with the opinions of a small town. Like most artists, she sometimes declares that she may give up photography because it is just too costly emotionally. But her declarations are unconvincing; her drive to make the pictures is palpable.

Malcolm Cowley observed of Faulkner that "he writes not what he wants to, but what he just has to write whether he wants to or not."[8] My own guess is that the drive toward artistic expression will prevail in Caffery. And come grinding season she'll be out in the fields because she likes the feel of it. "It is so cold, she said, "and there are so many smells swirling around. In the early morning dark I am happier in the fields than I would be anywhere else." Photography is her continuous means of asserting herself as a human being, as an agent in the world and not the subject of others' actions or opinions. It is her way to express the value and sense of life.

NOTES

For the insights of essayists not specifically cited in the notes, the author would like to acknowledge the following exhibition catalogues: *The Southern Voice: Terry Allen, Vernon Fisher, Ed McGowin*, The Fort Worth Art Museum, 1981; *Southern Eye, Southern Mind: A Photographic Inquiry*, The Memphis Academy of Arts, 1981; and *Southern Fictions*, Contemporary Arts Museum, Houston, 1983.

1. "Rip," *Houston Chronicle*, 1 Nov. 1989, sec. c., p. 1.

2. *Field and Foundry: A Working Contrast*, exhibition catalogue, Museum of Our National Heritage, Lexington, Massachusetts, 1987, unpaginated.

3. "Introduction," *The Portable Faulkner*, revised and expanded edition (London: Penguin Books, 1974), xx.

4. Unless otherwise noted, all quotes by Caffery are from an interview with the author on June 20, 1989.

5. "Close to Home: Seven Documentary Photographers," edited by David Featherstone, *Untitled 48*, Friends of Photography, San Francisco, 1989, p. 17.

6. Interview with author, September, 1989.

7. *Field and Foundry*.

8. *The Portable Faulkner*, xxiii–xxiv.

SUGAR FIELDS, WORKERS, AND NEIGHBORS

The photographs in this section, including some of Debbie Caffery's earliest, represent the main body of her work and chronicle the evolution of her style. Her photographs embody the culture of south Louisiana, especially its sugarcane workers. People are veiled, caught lying in the dirt, peering through a screen, hiding under a blanket, shrouded in smoke, backlit. Factories and machines take on eerie dimensions as sugar mills seem almost pulled skyward by dense steam, and the claws of cane loaders seem poised over the sugar mill, intent on attack.

Caffery took most of these photographs in the vicinity of Franklin and Patoutville, and many were exposed at sunrise. As her sense of composition and light matured, she was able to use to her advantage the mist hanging over the fields as the sun rose. The viewer sometimes wonders whether Caffery has revealed or hidden mysteries in the misty atmosphere and curling smoke that epitomize her photographs.

BALES OF BAGASSE, DECEMBER 1973

SCRAPING CANE, 1973

SUNRISE, 1974

PLANTERS, 1974

BA, 1974

REVEREND JOHN HARRIS, 1974

DEACON, 1974

MARY, 1974

UNTITLED (GIRL'S SOCKS AND SHOES), 1983

UNTITLED (MAN WITH CAP AND JOUTE), DECEMBER 1983

SUNRISE FIRE, DECEMBER 1984

PLANTER, 1984

HARRY'S HANDS, FEBRUARY 1984

ENTERPRISE, DECEMBER 1985

DARBY, 1985

UNTITLED (RABBIT), 1985

SUNSET—TRACTOR, DECEMBER 1985

TOWEL ON HAT, 1986

HOMER, 1986

HILTON, 1986

KOJACK AND HILTON, NOVEMBER 24, 1987

LEGS IN SMOKE, 1987

PINE NEEDLE FIRE, DECEMBER 1988

HOMAGE TO WILDCAT, DECEMBER 1988

PAYLOADER, DECEMBER 1988

KENNEDY, DECEMBER 1, 1988

BEFORE DAY, DECEMBER 1987

GARFISH, 1988

DUCKEGG, 1988

CANE TRUCK AT DAWN, DECEMBER 1988

BEFORE DAYBREAK, 1989

HOMER AND ROLAND, DECEMBER 15, 1985

ROLAND AND DOG, 1987

BACK OF KILGORE, NOVEMBER 14, 1988

DUMP WALL, 1989

UNDER THE WASH TABLE, 1989

NEIZAM AND FRIEND, 1989

PAPA, 1987

POLLY

Debbie Caffery met Polly, a woman of great dignity and simplicity, when her curiosity about a chair on the front porch of a lonesome house prompted her to approach the occupant. Their friendship has lasted for six years and represents on one level a search for understanding that could bridge two widely divergent cultures.

In the close confines of Polly's house, where light is scarce and precious, Caffery has explored with her camera the narrow spectrum between dim and dark. This series of photographs was important in Caffery's development as a photographer and represents a unique relationship between photographer and subject.

During the Christmas holidays of 1989, Polly moved from her house to a nursing home. She left behind her Bible with a page folded to an Old Testament verse, Lamentation for Princes. Caffery suggested that this was perhaps an unintended autobiographical revelation.

LOOKING AT ME, OCTOBER 25, 1984

FROM BEHIND, OCTOBER 29, 1984

ON HER BED, OCTOBER 29, 1984

REFLECTION IN MIRROR, NOVEMBER 7, 1984

HAND ON FACE, FEBRUARY 13, 1985

REFLECTION IN ARMOIRE MIRROR, MARCH 18, 1985

LACE DRESS, SUMMER 1985

SNAPPING HER FINGERS, DECEMBER 14, 1985

POLLY'S ARM ON HER SEWING MACHINE, 1989

CHICKEN IN FRONT OF SCREEN, MAY 2, 1986

CHICKEN IN HER LAP, 1986

POLLY HOLDING BLACKEYED SUSANS, MAY 28, 1986

HER HAND AND BLACKEYED SUSANS, MAY 28, 1986

POLLY NEXT TO PECAN TREE, MAY 28, 1986

BABY CHICKEN, MARCH 3, 1986

POLLY'S SLEEVE, 1988

EGGS, JANUARY 7, 1988

BOWL, SPOONS, FORK, 1987

BABY SHOES, 1988

LAMB, NOVEMBER 1987

SPIDER LILIES ON SEWING MACHINE, 1989

LAMENTATIONS FOR PRINCES, 1990

SHOOTING CLOSE TO HOME

Debbie and Clegg Caffery's three children—Joshua, Ruth, and Brennan— have become the subject of their mother's photography, as have other neighborhood children. At May Van's Camp, Caffery's exposure of children playing around a tree as she looked through a window produced an image that seems more tropical than even south Louisiana. This image contrasts vividly with that of the carefree young boy in the tire hurtling toward the bayou. Even with her children Caffery's sense of composition distinguishes her photographs. The final series of Joshua came after he was bitten by a snake (after being warned not to play with it). Sent to his room as discipline, he began painting his body and was discovered by his mother, who immediately saw an opportunity. These images of children project the youthful imagination of the subjects.

MAY VAN'S CAMP, SEPTEMBER 5, 1987

RUTH'S LEGS, 1984

RUTH FACING WALL, 1984

BOY WITH BLANKET, 1985

BRENNAN, 1989

BRENNAN AND RUTH, 1985

BRENNAN ARM OUT, 1987

CHILD WITH BALL, 1984

SUMMER, 1985

SLEEPING LIZARDS, 1986

JOSHUA, 1978

AFTER THE SNAKE BITE, 1983

AFTER THE SNAKE BITE, 1983

AFTER THE SNAKE BITE, 1983

AFTER THE SNAKE BITE, 1983

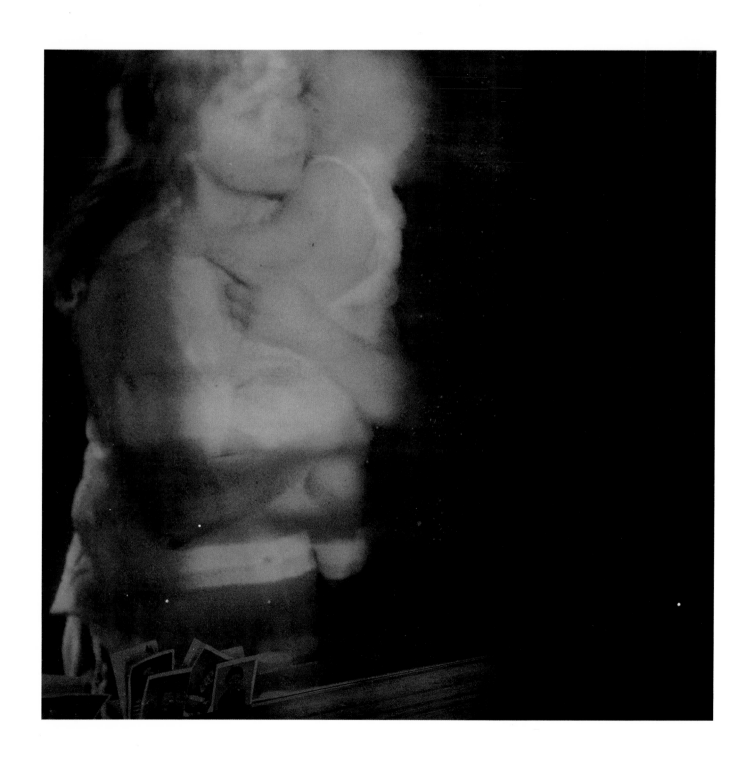

SELF PORTRAIT, 1981